a strange kinda heaven on some dark and sacred earth

thirteen short plays by
Brett Neveu

a strange kinda heaven on some dark and sacred earth

Thirteen short plays_by Brett Neveu

===============

THE AVON LADY

(It's 1976. JEAN and VONI sit at a kitchen table. JEAN is wearing a pantsuit and VONI is wearing slacks and a sweater. JEAN and VONI have coffee and look at various Avon products.)

(JEAN picks up a tube of lip balm.)

JEAN

This is nice. For a girl, this would be nice.

VONI

What's the string for?

JEAN

So she can wear it around her neck.

VONI

It smells like food. Won't somebody eat it because it smells like food?

JEAN

No.

VONI

Won't a dog or somebody's little brother eat it?

JEAN

Heavens no.

(VONI picks up a bottle. The bottle is shaped like a historical male figurine.)

JEAN (cont'd)

It's for the man.

(VONI picks up the bottle.

VONI

Aftershave?

JEAN
You're supposed to remove the head.

(VONI removes the top.)

JEAN (cont'd)
It's convenient and decorative.

VONI
It's spooky.

JEAN
It's not.

VONI
It's got no head.

JEAN
You're not supposed to leave the head off.

VONI
It's creepy.

JEAN
It's not creepy.

VONI
You don't think that if this thing was sitting on Yard's dresser and you woke up in the middle of the night, wouldn't you scream holy shit there's a headless doll on my husband's dresser?

JEAN
Of course not.

(VONI puts the head back on the bottle.)

VONI
Even with the head on its creepy.

JEAN
It's not aftershave. It's cologne. You called it aftershave before.

VONI
Aromatic.

JEAN

What?

VONI

Aroma-y.

JEAN

It's for the man.

(VONI picks up the bottle again, popping off the head.)

VONI

I'm the headless cologne doll! Look out or I'll stab out your eyeballs!

JEAN

That's not funny.

(VONI puts the bottle down. JEAN puts the head back on the bottle.)

VONI

Oh stop.

JEAN

You stop.

VONI

You stop.

JEAN

You're not helping.

VONI

I'm helping.

JEAN

Avon puts out a nice product.

VONI

I didn't say Avon didn't put out a nice product.

JEAN

Your tearing Avon doesn't help me.

VONI

--aw--

JEAN

When I'm with someone else now all I will be able to think about will be you pushing that headless bottle around and saying that its creepy and that it's going around stabbing my customer's eyes out. How can talk to other people with those sorts of pictures running around in my mind?

VONI

You won't have pictures like that.

JEAN

I can't have that sort of thing happening.

VONI

Block it out, push it away.

JEAN

Be supportive of Avon.

VONI

I am.

JEAN

And don't curse.

VONI

I didn't.

JEAN

When you were talking before about what it would be like if the cologne bottle was on Yard's dresser you said, "holy shit".

(A pause. JEAN holds up a tiny sample lipstick.)

JEAN (cont'd)

Did you see this new shade of lipstick?

VONI

No.

JEAN

It's called "Plum Dumpling".

VONI

Really? (laughs)

JEAN

What's the matter?

VONI

It's called "Plum Dumpling"?

JEAN

Yes.

VONI

That's sickening.

JEAN

It isn't.

VONI

"Dumpling"?

JEAN

What?

VONI

Like chicken dumplings?

JEAN

No.

VONI

What is going on with Avon, anyway?

JEAN

Nothing.

VONI

Avon has gotten so sickening lately.

JEAN

It has not!

VONI

Headless dolls and dumpling lipstick? That's real sickening!

JEAN

I thought you were going to stop it?!

VONI

Hey, you're the one that presented me with "Plum Dumpling" lipstick!

JEAN

You're the one that said that dogs and children are going to want to eat my lip balm!

VONI

Well, they might want to!

JEAN

Help me…

(JEAN begins to cry.)

VONI

Oh oh oh oh, stop stop stop stop --

JEAN

I'm sorry, Voni, I'm sorry --

VONI

Shh shh shh -- why are you sorry?

JEAN

You're right! Avon <u>is</u> disgusting! What is this junky stuff anyhow!?!

VONI

I was just teasing! It's nice. It's not junky.

JEAN

It's not! It's weird! It's strange! It's sick!

VONI

It's not any of those things --

JEAN

Look at the catalog --

(JEAN opens a small Avon catalog.)

JEAN

-- look here -- it's a dinosaur bubble-bath! Dinosaurs! Don't you think dinosaurs are ugly?! Don't you think dinosaurs are stupid?! Don't you hate them?! Don't you hate dinosaurs?!

VONI

Dinosaurs are fine.

JEAN

Don't you think dinosaurs are stupid?!

VONI

They aren't.

JEAN

But don't you think it's true? Don't you think it's all so sickening?

VONI

It's not. It's not sickening.

JEAN

Don't you think you were right?

VONI

Everything you sell for Avon is just fine.

JEAN

But isn't it sickening?

VONI

It's fine.

JEAN

Isn't it ugly?

VONI

No.

JEAN

Don't you hate it?

VONI

I don't.

JEAN

You like dinosaurs?

VONI

I suppose.

JEAN

You like bubble-bath?

VONI

I guess.

JEAN

So you like these dinosaur bubble-baths?

VONI

They're okay.

JEAN

They're not sickening?

VONI

They're fine.

JEAN

The dinosaur bubble-baths come in three styles -- Brontosaurus, Triceratops and Tyrannosaurus Rex.

VONI

That's nice.

JEAN

There's the giant long-tailed plant-eating Brontosaurus, the pointy-faced sweetheart of the jungle the Triceratops and the fearsome and toothy Tyrannosaurus Rex.

VONI

Good.

JEAN
All three dinosaur bubble baths are a bathtub friendly size and are each made out of water-proof polymers. You love dinosaurs, right?

VONI
I never said that I loved dinosaurs.

JEAN
Do you hate dinosaurs?

VONI
I don't have a huge opinion of dinosaurs either way.

JEAN
You don't have to have a huge opinion of dinosaurs?

VONI
No.

JEAN
How about dinosaur bubble baths?

VONI
I don't see myself owning a dinosaur bubble bath, if that's what you're asking.

JEAN
Not even the sweetheart of the jungle, Triceratops? (pause) How do you feel about a golden Liberty Bell with cologne inside? You could give it to Kendall for his birthday.

VONI
No.

JEAN
Doesn't Kendall have a birthday coming up?

VONI
What is going on?

JEAN
Going on?

VONI

Were you even really crying before?

JEAN

When?

VONI

When you were upset about what I said?

JEAN

I was really crying. But I mostly only cried in order to calm you down.

VONI

You manipulated me?

JEAN

No. It was only friendly mutual agreement through the use of proper equivocating. (beat) Is there more coffee?

VONI

No.

JEAN

There isn't?

VONI

No.

JEAN

I know there's more in there. I saw it.

VONI

How could you see through the percolator?

JEAN

I felt it then, when I poured.

VONI

I'm sure it's gone cold.

JEAN

I'm sure it hasn't.

VONI

It has.

JEAN

Couldn't you warm it again?

VONI

Not really, no.

JEAN

I'm sorry if you think I manipulated you. I should tell you something. What I was doing? Crying like that? It was a sales technique.

VONI

Crying was a sales technique?

JEAN

It's an Avon Lady sales technique.

VONI

Avon encourages crying?

JEAN

Crying is recommended in certain situations.

VONI

Which situations?

JEAN

Situations with close friends. That refuse to buy Avon products.

VONI

I didn't refuse to buy.

JEAN

You were on the path to refusal by making fun of Avon products.

VONI

So you cried?

JEAN

Sort of.

VONI
That's awful.

JEAN
I know.

VONI
And it's awful that Avon says you should cry.

JEAN
Avon only states I should cry at friends. An Avon Lady should never cry at acquaintances or neighbors she barely knows.

VONI
Are you required to cry when a friend may refuse to buy Avon products?

JEAN
Actually, I only pretended to cry at you. I didn't really cry.

VONI
So are you required to pretend to cry?

JEAN
It's actually only recommended that I cry, but it's also recommended that I don't pretend, that I actually cry. But I couldn't bring myself to actually cry.

VONI
I don't like any of this.

JEAN
Why not?

VONI
I don't like this manipulation of friends. This manipulation of neighbors.

JEAN
It's not really like that. Avon is just regular conversation, but with an added purchasing layer thrown in.

VONI
Is that right?

JEAN

Yes. It's as if I were over here having coffee with you as I would do normally on a Wednesday, both of us telling each other terrible tales regarding our lives, hopeless over -the-fence anecdotes and god-awful grocery-store related-cattiness -- but with the added interesting element of lovely make-up sales.

VONI

But it twists it all up, don't you think?

JEAN

It twists it?

VONI

It makes me into someone for manipulating and you into a manipulator.

JEAN

That hasn't changed, actually, from before.

VONI

Oh yeah?

JEAN

Before, when we would have coffee, I was the manipulator then also.

VONI

You were?

JEAN

I would often tell you things about people that were untrue. I would pretend to cry. I would laugh even though I didn't think what you were saying was very funny.

VONI

That wasn't very nice of you to do.

JEAN

I didn't mean it.

VONI

You didn't mean it?

JEAN

No, but I agree, it wasn't nice.

VONI

It wasn't.

JEAN

But don't you think since I've told you honestly all the things I used to do and that I've also confessed that, yes, Avon requires me to be awful to my closest friends in order to try to sell them products, don't you think my revealing those secrets, my personal secrets, don't you think that my opening up to you is worth something?

VONI

I suppose.

JEAN

So that we can now have a normal conversation now that the air is clear?

VONI

I'm not sure.

JEAN

But haven't I been so honest?

VONI

Unless your honesty is another Avon sales technique.

JEAN

Actually. It is.

VONI

It is?

JEAN

You've caught me. Avon recommends that once an Avon Lady is caught within your intended covert sales activity, that she, before she gets kicked out of her friend's home, that she come clean and let the friend know what kind of lies they've been dealing in, what kind of trickery has been afoot. But it's a good suggestion, isn't it? Honesty? It's not like the other suggestion, the other suggestion -- lying. It's better than that, isn't it?

VONI

Yes.

JEAN

So I'll be good now.

VONI

I'm not sure --

JEAN

You don't have to buy a single thing.

VONI

I don't?

JEAN

I'll be a better friend now, I'll not fake-laugh or fake-cry. I'll both laugh and cry for real when I feel either are appropriate.

VONI

Don't feel like you need to.

JEAN

You were right before, you were right. "Plum Dumpling" is really, really sickening.

VONI

It is sickening.

JEAN

Sick.

VONI

Yuck.

JEAN

It's nice to be here with you, talking, sharing.

VONI

I guess so.

JEAN

We're not lying. We're being real to each other.

VONI

Yes.

JEAN

And if you really wanted anything from the catalog, not that I'm asking or manipulating or doing anything that's recommended Avon Ladies do, but if you wanted anything from the catalog that you might find interesting, now its not tainted. Now it would be an honest purchase. An honest purchase from an honest place.

VONI

Are you still trying to sell me Avon?

JEAN

No. I'm not. I'm only being sincere.

VONI

Listen! I don't want any of your sickening Avon products!

JEAN

Exactly. Why would you?

VONI

Exactly.

JEAN

Why not buy Avon to help a friend who is just trying to make a little money on the side?

VONI

That's just great.

JEAN

Everyone in the neighborhood will find out you didn't buy Avon and they will hate you.

VONI

That's just wonderful.

JEAN

If you buy Avon then Jesus will love you.

VONI

That's just perfect.

JEAN

Everyone everywhere is buying Avon.

VONI

Oh yeah?

JEAN

You're my best friend.

VONI

Am I?

JEAN

You're mean!

VONI

And now you're hurt.

JEAN

Yes.

VONI

Good.

JEAN

You like that I'm hurt?

VONI

Yes.

JEAN

You're cruel.

VONI

I'm not. You are. You're cruel. Really, really, cruel. Really, really, very, very cruel.

(A pause.)

JEAN

I swear Kendall would like that Liberty Bell cologne. And then you don't even have to go shopping for him. Just pick it out of the catalog and in a few weeks your order comes in and I bring to your house, giftwrapped and everything. It'll all be taken care of.

VONI

Oh yeah?

JEAN

Yes.

VONI

Okay.

JEAN

Really?

VONI

Sure. Why not.

JEAN

Super! I'll put you down for one! I swear he'll love it.

(JEAN writes down the order. A pause.)

VONI

You want some more coffee?

JEAN

I thought it had gone cold.

VONI

I can warm it.

JEAN

Okay.

(A pause.)

VONI

Do you want a cigarette?

JEAN

Yes.

(VONI and JEAN light cigarettes. JEAN finds an ashtray. A pause as VONI and JEAN smoke.)

JEAN (cont'd) (cont'd)

What time is it?

(VONI squints at a clock someplace.)

VONI

It's ten-fifteen.

JEAN

Ten-fifteen?

VONI

Yeah.

JEAN

What a glorious day.

(They smoke.)

(Lights fade.)

END

HOLA, AMIGO

(Lights up. KIM, a nicely dressed woman in her late thirties, sits at a bar with GARY, a well-groomed fiftish man in a gray suit. KIM has had a glass of wine and GARY sips on a tall glass of soda.)

KIM

I know that I love you and I'm trying to understand if you love me.

GARY

I'm just not sure of a lot of things.

KIM

What do you mean? What does that mean you're not sure? I thought we were in love. That's what I thought, that both of us were in love. I'm not sure what to say. Am I wrong? Was I not understanding where we were?

GARY

I'm not sure.

KIM

You're not sure if you're in love with me?

GARY

I'm not sure about things with us.

KIM

You can't not be sure if you're in love or not. Either you're in love with me or something else's going on. You have to explain it to me or I won't know what you mean. I can't go around thinking certain things about us when I'm completely wrong and you have all the answers. I feel angry and stupid. It doesn't make me feel good.

GARY

You feel sick?

KIM

No.

GARY

Oh. (laughs)

KIM

What?

GARY

I was joking.

KIM

You were joking about what?

GARY

You said you didn't feel good, and I asked if you were sick. (pause) I'm just trying to make things clear.

KIM

Making what things clear?

GARY

It was a joke. It's no problem or anything.

KIM

I didn't think it was any problem.

GARY

Do you want another glass of wine?

KIM

That's all right.

GARY

Okay.

KIM

It is just that when I was younger everybody treated me a certain way. They would tell me… Oh… I'm not sure. But they would treat me a certain way and it always would make me upset. I'm still treated the same way. I don't want to be treated that way.

GARY

I'm not treating you any way.

KIM

I just don't want to fall out of love.

GARY

It's all right.

KIM

What's all right?

GARY

This.

KIM

Us?

GARY

Yeah.

KIM

Except you're not in love.

GARY

Hm.

KIM

Do you have a cigarette?

GARY

Uh. No.

KIM

I'm not really smoking again, I was just needing one.

GARY

Oh.

KIM

I'm still not smoking.

GARY

Good.

KIM

I'd been smoking a long time.

GARY

I know.

KIM

I've quit.

(GARY finds a cigarette in his jacket pocket.)

GARY

Here you go.

KIM

Great.

(KIM puts the cigarette in her mouth. She finds some matches and lights it. She smokes.)

(A long pause.)

(TIM enters he has a margarita in his hand. He wears a suit with a loosened tie.)

KIM

Hola, Amigo!

TIM

Hey, Kim.

KIM

A margarita.

TIM

Yep.

KIM

Do you know Gary?

TIM

No.

GARY

Hey.

KIM

(to GARY) This is Tim.

TIM

(to GARY) I think we rode up the elevator together today.

GARY

You're right.

KIM

Gary's one of the lawyers in my office.

TIM

I work on 24.

KIM

(to TIM) How are you?

TIM

Am I too early for Cinco de Mayo?

KIM

I'm not sure.

TIM

I don't think so.

KIM

How is the margarita?

TIM

It's all right. It's good.

KIM

Great.

TIM

Did you want one?

KIM

That's okay.

TIM

They're good.

KIM

I'm allergic to tequila.

TIM

Really?

KIM

I get really sick. I feel horrible if I drink it.

TIM

Wow. Is it from what it's made from?

KIM

I'm not sure.

TIM

Huh. (pause) Nice meeting you, Gary.

GARY

Yeah.

(TIM exits.)

KIM

I just want to be with you and I know you think that's wrong.

GARY

No.

KIM

I know that you see me in a certain way, and I don't want to be treated that way.

GARY

I know.

KIM

I just want to be clear.

GARY

Sure.

KIM

Good.

GARY

I should get back upstairs.

KIM

Okay.

GARY

I'll see you tomorrow.

KIM

Okay.

(GARY gives KIM a long kiss.)

(GARY exits. KIM sits. A pause. She picks up her purse and pulls out a pack of cigarettes. She takes one out and lights it. She smokes. Lights fade to black.)

END

FIREPLACE FIRE

(Lights up. CAL and VERNON stand at a street corner. CAL wears a baseball cap.)

CAL

Gasoline.

VERNON

That'd seem to burn too heavy.

CAL

It's just to get goin'.

VERNON

Twist-ups work.

CAL

Unless you wanna hot one right off.

VERNON

Just to get it started, twist-ups is fine.

CAL

I don't wanna fool with twist-ups.

VERNON

Twist-up paper don't have too much foolin'.

CAL

I'm done with the paper way.

VERNON

Yer gonna set the whole damn thing up usin' gas.

CAL

Nah. I pre-soak.

VERNON

What, the wood?

CAL

Pre-soak the individual logs.

VERNON

How you pre-soak?

CAL

In a vat.

VERNON

A vat where?

CAL

Out backa my place, back of the fence.

VERNON

You gotta vat of gas sittin' back of your fence?

CAL

Yeah, just for soakin'.

VERNON

The thing could go up like a bomb sometime.

CAL

I got a sheet of tin over top.

VERNON

Don't matter with fumes the thing could go.

CAL

It's fulla logs so it's not gonna go noplace.

VERNON

Logs don't make fumes stop.

CAL

I use tongs to pull the logs when I need to get 'em.

VERNON

Tongs ain't gonna stop the fumes neither.

CAL

You're just peeved cuz you didn't think to do it.

VERNON

I ain't doin' no log-filled gas-vat out the back of my house.

CAL

Yeah, I bet you run home and do it in about a minute.

VERNON

Stupidest thing.

CAL

It saves time and money.

VERNON

Twist-ups do the same thing without the threat of fire and explosion.

CAL

Twist-ups are for children. I gotta new way and it's the way of the future and you just can't seem to get that.

VERNON

I just ain't ready to give my life for a fireplace fire.

CAL

Then you ain't willin' to live your damn life to the max. Gotta live life the max, Vernon, or you might as well sit on a box, age-up fast and quick-die backwards into the drink.

(A pause. VERNON removes his cap.)

(Lights out.)

END

TWO WOMEN ON THE TRAIN TALKING ABOUT DEPRESSION

(Lights fade up.)

(Two women enter. BARB and JANET. They are in mid-conversation. They board a commuter train.)

BARB

Oh, yes.

JANET

Me too.

BARB

Do you ever cry on the train?

JANET

I have. It's strange.

BARB

When I cried, people looked at me.

JANET

Yeah.

BARB

They just looked at me like I was strange.

JANET

No one talks to you though.

BARB

No. They were just looking.

(The train begins moving. It stops and starts throughout.)

JANET

It would be nice if someone said, "Are you okay?"

BARB

I suppose they may have not known I was crying. I had my head down sort of. I was sort of in a ball or maybe it looked like I was sleeping. I'm sure it looked strange.

JANET

But it's very good to do. I've seen people crying on the train. People walking down the street crying. People crying at Taco Bell.

BARB

It can really help, though.

JANET

I mean you're at work and it's like you're living a double life.

BARB

Right.

JANET

Like you're living two lives.

BARB

Right.

JANET

There's "work you" and then "when you're alone you". Like when you're at home alone.

BARB

I know.

JANET

You can't let it out at work. You have to hold the whole thing in.

BARB

That's hard.

JANET

All day long just at your desk. When you're alone, then it's like, "Well, here I am."

BARB

So, do you live alone?

JANET

Yes.

BARB

I live alone, too. I mean, you get home and there's no one else there.

JANET

I know. It's like you have to change who you are when you get to work.

BARB

Suddenly there are all these people. When you're at work you have to be around them.

JANET

Living by yourself is not easy.

BARB

Sundays are hard.

JANET

My brother lived alone for a year. I mean all alone. He quit his job and just sat in his apartment alone for a year. He never even asked anyone to come visit him.

BARB

Was he okay?

JANET

He just needed to be alone. He was very depressed.

BARB

My brother thought he was depressed for a year but he just had T.B.

JANET

Really?

BARB

He didn't know he had T.B., but he was so down and then he went to the doctor and found out he had T.B..

JANET

He didn't know he had T.B.?

BARB

And they had to monitor him for a year after that just to see where he got the T.B. and they found out that he had gotten it from a bird in his attic.

JANET

Really.

BARB

He was up there trying to catch a squirrel that was in his attic and he leaned his hand on a window sill and there was a bird nest there and he just leaned into it wrong and that's where the doctor said he got T.B..

JANET

Oh wow.

BARB

He's okay now. He's very happy. He was just here visiting a couple of weeks ago.

JANET

Really?

BARB

We went to dinner and to the museum.

JANET

My brother is on some medication now.

BARB

Oh?

JANET

I don't know what it is, not prozac, but something like it.

BARB

Like a lower dose?

JANET

No, like something like prozac but something different.

BARB

I wonder what it is.

JANET
It's like midlac or jantec? Something like it. He's on it.

BARB
And he's doing okay?

JANET
He's doing okay. He's three years younger than me.

BARB
Oh.

JANET
He still gets very down. It's just sad sometimes for him.

BARB
Yeah.

JANET
He gets these headaches. He gets migraines.

BARB
Ooo, ouch.

JANET
He just has to sit when he gets them.

BARB
My aunt gets migraines so bad that sometimes they make her throw up.

JANET
His don't usually make him throw up.

BARB
Are they migraines or are they just bad headaches?

JANET
They're migraines.

BARB
Is he sure? They might just be really bad headaches.

JANET

Isn't that what a migraine is?

BARB

I guess you're right.

JANET

He gets these migraines and he just sits until they're gone.

BARB

Has he told his doctor about them?

JANET

He can't take any medicine for them because of the medicine he's already on.

BARB

Can he take aspirin?

JANET

For a migraine?

BARB

I guess they wouldn't help a migraine much.

JANET

It's his therapist that has him on the other medication, so he can't really do anything about the migraines.

BARB

Is his therapy going well for him?

JANET

Yes.

BARB

It's helping?

JANET

Yes. He's doing better.

BARB

It probably helps.

JANET

I should try that sometime.

BARB

Therapy?

JANET

I mean, everyone should go sometime.

BARB

I know.

JANET

Can you believe I work for The School of Psychotherapy, and I've never been to see a therapist?

BARB

I think that it would be a good idea just to go to get some of that stuff out.

JANET

We build up so much stuff. In our minds.

BARB

It's just in today's society, there's no where to go with problems.

JANET

I know. I don't know what to do half the time.

BARB

I've been looking at some of those books about problems.

JANET

I've seen some books like that.

BARB

Some of the books that you see telling you to deal with your "spiritual self".

JANET

Right.

BARB
I don't know much about my "spiritual self".

JANET
Yeah.

BARB
I went to church when I was young, but I don't think that's what they mean.

JANET
It's confusing as a child. It's like your spiritual child-self, and that's confusing.

BARB
These books talk about finding the spirit within you so you can achieve all those things you want to achieve.

JANET
Yeah.

BARB
There was one that said something about taking ancient Native American philosophies and using them in your day to day life.

JANET
Really?

BARB
I really didn't look at it that much but I think that you are supposed to let things take there course or something or something about your inner spirit. While you're at work
you're supposed to feel freedom or when you get frustrated with your computer, you're supposed to do something else. I forget what it said exactly.

JANET
Oh.

BARB
There were a couple of other books. There was one about finding the naughty child inside you.

(BARB and JANET laugh.)

JANET
I've heard about that one. The naughty child within you. It releases you.

BARB
Yeah.

JANET
I need to look at some of those books.

BARB
Yeah.

JANET
Yeah. Where did you see those?

BARB
The bookstore. I went over to the bookstore over lunch.

JANET
I should do that.

BARB
Those types of books are there.

JANET
I should do some reading.

BARB
I know. I try to read.

JANET
I do, too. Sometimes I just get stuck in front of the T.V., though.

BARB
Yeah.

JANET
Do you ever watch The Appraisers?

BARB
The what?

JANET

The Appraisers.

BARB

I don't think so.

JANET

It's the show where people bring something on and then appraisers tell them how much the thing they brought on is worth.

BARB

Oh -- I think I have seen that show.

JANET

I love that show!

BARB

I've seen it a couple of times. I can never remember when it's on.

JANET

It's on every Friday at 8:00.

BARB

Oh.

JANET

I was watching once and they had a sword on there that the owner said he used to cut watermelon with and the sword was appraised at $30,000!

BARB

Wow.

JANET

It was amazing! I just love that show. And then they had this woman on that had this chair that she thought was very old, I mean, it looked very old and was some sort of rare style, so she brought it in to The Appraisers. The gentleman who was looking at it was so nice and was trying very hard not to hurt her feelings, so he told her about the chair at first as if it weren't a fake, telling her about the style and the make. Then he said, "One of the things I like about this job is telling people that they have found a treasure. This chair, on today's market, could fetch $400,000." Then he paused. Then he said, "But this is the part of my job that I don't like very well at all. The chair is a forgery." Then he told her why. The legs were wrong. The back was wrong. The seat was worn away with paint thinner instead of age. She was upset, thinking she had been ripped off. But the appraiser asked her how much she paid for it. She said $600. He told her it was such a good forgery that she could sell it for $2000. That's not too bad.

BARB

No.

JANET

I just love that show.

BARB

I've seen it before. Not recently, though.

JANET

It gets me out of a funk.

BARB

I'm thinking of going to a doctor.

JANET

A medical doctor?

BARB

Maybe.

JANET

Are you sick?

BARB

I'm not sure.

JANET

That guy that owned that really great expensive sword? I read recently that he had a stroke.

BARB

Where did you hear that?

JANET

I don't know. But I think it's great he found out about that $30,000 sword before he had a stroke.

(The train stops at JANET's stop. JANET gets out of the train.)

JANET (cont'd)

Well, bye! See you tomorrow!

BARB

Okay, I'll see you at the building tomorrow.

JANET

Bye!

BARB

Bye.

(JANET exits. BARB smiles. Her smile slowly fades.)

(Lights fade to black.)

END

FOUR FATAL FLAWS IN YELLOW PAGE ADVERTISING

(Dim light up on JERRY and WALTER. JERRY, seated on a bar stool and wearing faded red sweats, sips on a beer from a mug. WALTER, in shirt and tie, holds a clipboard and has a pencil behind his ear.)

WALTER

No drinking.

JERRY

Aw.

WALTER

Can ya just wait until I'm through?

JERRY

It's a sippin' beer.

WALTER

I just don't wanna hear gulps in your fucking throat.

JERRY

I just said I'm sippin' it!

WALTER

You never fucking sipped a fucking beezo in your life!

JERRY

I'll make an accordance for your seminar presentation.

WALTER

And don't ask me in the middle --

JERRY

Just get on with the goddamn thing, huh?

WALTER

-- don't fucking ask me in the middle for a second beezo 'cause I ain't poppin' a beezo while I'm giving my fucking seminar.

(JERRY takes a gulp of beer.)

WALTER
And see you fucking gulped it.

(JERRY belches.)

WALTER
Act like I need you to act.

JERRY
Don't think I don't want success for you, okay? I want only just the best for you outa life and if you don't believe that then fuck you 'till it hurts.

(A long pause.)

WALTER
You like the new set up? The stools, new back of the bar and you see the mini-fridge? No more ice chest. Maggie wanted a rack above for wine glasses, too, so that's on back order.

JERRY
Swell fucking set up, Walt.

WALTER
Better'n dad's by a country mile.

JERRY
Yeah, dad's fucking basement bar always smelled like fucking laundry and fucking mildew.

WALTER
Not mine. Mine's got fucking ambiance. Mine gives me fucking clues about life. Fucking clues about life betterment and willpower and shit.

JERRY
Damn great bar, Walt.

(JERRY gulps his beer.)

WALTER
Goddamnit, Jerry. Stop gulping your fucking beer.

JERRY
I gotta be back to the pool by three.

WALTER

Mm.

(JERRY belches.)

WALTER

Okay. Now. You're a prospective yellow pages ad buyer. You're listening to my seminar. When my seminar is over, feel free to pepper me with questions.

JERRY

Done.

WALTER

So. Gimme a sip of that beer.

(JERRY hands WALTER his beer. WALTER takes a sip.)

WALTER

Bottoms of my feet hurt goddamnit.

JERRY

Take a breath or some shit. Shake it off.

WALTER

Fuck you I'm fine. (pause) Okay. So. Prospective buyer of yellow page advertising space. How are you doin' today?

JERRY

Better'n fuck.

WALTER

C'mon, Jerry, nobody's fucking gonna say "better'n fuck."

JERRY

Then, what, uh. I'm doing just fine.

WALTER

Okay. Good. I'm here today to tell you about the Four Fatal Flaws in Yellow Page Advertising. Since you're thinking of advertising in our local yellow page section of our telephone book, since you've decided to put your advertising dollars for your company to work in the yellow pages, I'm talking to you today to tell you how to make those dollars work best for you in the best way possible. So that you get the most out of your advertising. It's what you've come to this seminar for. To learn how to get the most out of your ad dollars. And so. The first fatal flaw of yellow page advertising is... *Bad Placement Choices.*

JERRY

No shit?

WALTER

Goddamnit Jerry!

JERRY

What the fuck stop yelling at fucking me!

WALTER

Nobody's gonna say "no shit!"

JERRY

You really think that keeping stopping to control whatever the fuck I say is a good idea 'cause the way I think is that anybody could say anything at any moment during your goddamn seminar so you gotta be prepared for people to say all sort of fucking things and if you ain't prepared for that then you might as well walk the fuck back to the Pamida and kiss Marty Mitchum's ass and tell him you couldn't do shit 'cause you was too sensitive to human communication that didn't agree with your set fucking format!

(A pause.)

WALTER

You're right.

JERRY

Then walk it the fuck off and tell me more about Bad fucking Placement Choices.

WALTER

All right. Okay. Okay. (long pause) Sip of that beer?

(JERRY sips WALTER's beer.)

JERRY

Go.

WALTER

Okay. *Bad Placement Choices*. If you, the advertising buyer, just throw out any term, Yellow Pages will maybe mess up the placement. Choosing where to place your advertisement is not the slam-dunk it might look to be. For example, air conditioning services could be listen under: Heating and Cooling Contractors, Air Conditioning Contractors and Systems or Air Conditioning Equipment & Systems-Repairing. Or even other ones.

JERRY

Huh.

WALTER

So make sure you muli-list and I also suggest you advertise horizontally for broader exposure. Okay. The number two fatal flaw is: *Terrible Advertising Copy*. Don't let your name be how you sell stuff. "Ray's Extermination" isn't gonna tell anybody anything. You got to bullet-point your services. Say stuff like "We kill roaches." Or "We'll get the rats from your walls." Or "We use the most high-tech devices to rid your house of the most feral of raccoons."

(JERRY laughs.)

JERRY

That made me laugh.

WALTER

(smiling) Humor sells.

JERRY

Raccoons.

WALTER

Number three fatal flaw of yellow page advertising: *Junky Design in your Advertisement*. You know the ads I'm talking about -- some map or a clown or a dollar bill or something stupid like that. It's meaningless. Include more blank space so the eye can focus. And if you can, include a drawing that is pertinent to you what you're selling. I mean, look at Denny's -- they have drawings of their food right inside their menus.

Makes you want the food even more after you seen it drawn out, am I wrong?

(JERRY shakes his head.)

WALTER

And fatal flaw number four: *Track Your Results*. How you gonna know if your ad dollars are working if you don't check to make sure your ad dollars are working? Ask people when they call or come in where they happened to hear about your business. If you follow my seminar's advice, then nine times out of ten I bet they say "I read about you in the yellow pages!" And that's my solemn guarantee. Your ad dollars will work for you, not the other way around if you heed my warnings about the Four Fatal Flaws of Yellow Page Advertising. So that's it. Thank you and good night.

(A pause.)

JERRY

Well that's just great. Plain talk for plain folk.

WALTER

It's a two hour seminar. I imagine I'll say what I just said and then be peppered with questions with the remaining (checks watch) hour and fifty minutes. (pause) You got any questions you wanna toss at me?

JERRY

Not really.

WALTER

I was thinking, too, that maybe I'd branch out and say that the Four Fatal Flaws of Yellow Page Advertising applied to life choices, too, you know?

JERRY

Yeah?

WALTER

Like, okay -- the first one -- *Bad Placement*. That's about intentionally putting yourself in a bad situation. It fucks up everything. And the second one -- *Terrible Copy*? That's just people telling other folk not just their names, but opening up to who they really are, inside. And number three -- *Junky Design*. I mean, dress nice! Buy some new pants. Get a hair cut. Treat yourself like you're somebody and not a nothing. And the last one: *Track Your Results*. Are positive changes in you creating positive results in your existence and those that exist around you? Make a note of it if they are and certainly note it if your results are causing harm or not playing out in ways you would like. See? It all applies to everyday life, too. I got a shitload to talk about. A fucking shitload. People are gonna see a fucking brilliant light. (pause) It's a whole new me, Jerry. New like fucking right out of the box. The day is dawning, the sunrise is spliting over the crest of the horizon. Fucking sky full of diamonds.

(JERRY holds up his glass.)

JERRY

Here's to you.

WALTER

Yeah. Here's fucking (makes a fist) *to me*.

(JERRY sips his beer. WALTER, lost in the dreams of his own wondrous future, looks toward the heavens, his smile growing ever larger. Lights fade.)

END

ETHNIC CLEANSING DAY

(Lights up. It is summer. KENT, wearing shorts and a T-shirt, relaxes in a recliner. MATT, in shorts and a brightly colored button-up shirt, sits on a wooden dining chair nearby, a plastic shopping bag at his feet. Both MATT and KENT take sips from open cans of Coke.)

KENT

Where did you go specifically?

MATT

Cronulla.

KENT

Where is that?

MATT

The southeastern part of the country.

KENT

The whole place must have taken you awhile to get to.

MATT

It's a long flight and then there's a drive out.

KENT

Did you sit next to anybody interesting on the plane?

MATT

Nobody was next to me. I had three seats to myself.

KENT

Traveling alone can be rough.

MATT

It was alright.

KENT

What sort of stuff did you do down there?

MATT

I went to the beach.

KENT

Was it a big beach?

MATT

I was.

KENT

Did you meet anyone down there to hang out with?

MATT

I met a group of guys at my hotel's bar/pub.

KENT

A few laid back sorts? A group of drinking pals?

MATT

Just some guys.

KENT

What were they like?

MATT

Alright.

KENT

Rowdy?

MATT

Not really.

KENT

Hooligans? Like those friends you had in high school?

MATT

No.

KENT

Like Chad Rascola?

MATT

No.

KENT

Like Chuck Baird?

MATT

No.

KENT

Chuck was a drinker.

MATT

He didn't drink all the time.

KENT

He had those home-made tatoos on his hands. (pause) What kinds of places did you go to down there?

MATT

Clubs and nightclubs and other bar/pubs and the beach.

KENT

Sounds like good time down under. Aussie lager and barbecues.

MATT

It was fun.

KENT

Lots of girls?

MATT

Yeah.

KENT

"Shielas?"

MATT

I guess.

KENT

Are those Australian "Shielas" fun?

MATT

I guess so.

KENT

So you hung out with fun "Shielas" and rowdy guys down at the beach and at the local bars. What was the name of the beach you mostly went to?

MATT

Royal National Park Beach.

KENT

Royal National Park Beach? Did you bring your camera?

MATT

I have some pictures.

KENT

You brought your camera?

(MATT pulls a small stack of pictures from the plastic bag.)

KENT (cont'd)

You didn't take that many.

MATT

I'm not the one who took the pictures.

KENT

You didn't bring your camera? Who took these pictures?

MATT

One of the guys I met. Marcus.

KENT

He mailed them to you?

MATT

He e-mailed them to me and I printed them off.

KENT

Great. Let's take a look.

(MATT hands KENT the small stack of pictures.)

KENT (cont'd)

Can you go through and tell me what these are mostly of? (looking at the first one) What's this?

MATT

That's me and Teddy.

KENT

Teddy?

MATT

He's one of the guys down there.

KENT

Where's this taken?

MATT

The beach by where I was staying.

KENT

Royal National Beach?

MATT

Yeah.

KENT

Who's that?

MATT

Courtney.

KENT

That's one of the shielas? She's really pretty. Is she your new Aussie girlfriend? (laughs) There's a lot of people on the beach.

MATT

It was crowded.

KENT
It's really crowded. Look at everyone.

(KENT moves on to the next picture, pulling at the corner of the others.)

KENT (cont'd)
You only have about five or six pictures? You shouldn't have forgot your camera. That camera would have been great to have down there. You could have taken pictures of the landscape and all sorts of things. Then you would certainly have more than five or six pictures. You could have taken pictures of all sorts of stuff. (looks at the picture) What's this?

MATT
That's the ocean.

KENT
Is this taken from the beach? Is this morning or evening?

MATT
Morning.

KENT
This is a nice photo. Marcus did a good job. What a beautiful picture. You really should have brought your camera. You take a trip like this and you should always bring a camera or at least buy a disposable camera. Then you'd end up with some great shots of your own. (moves onto the next picture) Is this another crowd?

MATT
It's the same crowd.

KENT
They seem closer together. Is this a picture of you? Where are you in this picture?

MATT
(points at picture) I'm way back there.

KENT
Why did Marcus send you this picture?

MATT
He e-mailed me what he took.

KENT
I don't understand why he only took five or six pictures.

MATT
He wasn't a big photographer or anything.

KENT
Still. It isn't many. (looks more closely at picture) Is that a fight? These people there, are they fighting?

MATT
They're fist-fighting.

KENT
Why are they fist-fighting? (moves onto the next picture) What's going on here?

MATT
More fist-fighting.

KENT
Are all of these pictures of fighting?

(KENT shuffles through the remaining pictures.)

MATT
Not the first three.

(KENT settles on one of the pictures. He looks at it for a bit.)

MATT (cont'd)
That guy was Lebanese.

KENT
Who was Lebanese?

MATT
That guy right there who's in the middle of it.

KENT

(points at picture) Is that you?

MATT

Yes.

KENT

What are you doing?

MATT

Hitting him.

KENT

What's everybody doing?

MATT

Fighting. (beat) Marcus posted these pictures on this one website on the internet. (pause) Eventually about thirty guys were beating that Lebanese guy. He was okay in the end, though. Afterwards the group of us went through the crowd looking for more Lebanese guys and when we found someone who was Lebanese we beat him up. In the end we beat up about ten or eleven guys. Then we heard that two Lebanese guys jumped a lifeguard. The Lebanese guys had pulled the lifeguard off his lifeguard stand and shoved his face in the sand. We heard about that and made it over to where that had happened and we found the Lebanese guys and jumped them and I hit one of them in the face with a bottle. The Lebanese guys then ran off down the street, a few of the guys I was with running after them, the Lebanese guy's faces bloody and blood running down their arms. I don't know if the guys I met caught them eventually or not.

(A pause.)

KENT

You should see if those pictures can come off the internet. Especially this one.

(KENT holds up one of the pictures.)

MATT

I bought those sunglasses when I was down there.

(KENT hands the pictures back to MATT. A pause.)

KENT
Hey. You want to take April for a walk around the neighborhood?

MATT
If you want me to, sure.

KENT
Her leash and collar are in the garage.

(MATT puts the pictures into the plastic bag.)

KENT (cont'd)
I'll wait here to help your mom when she gets back with the groceries.

MATT
Okay.

KENT
On your way out put those pictures back in your car.

MATT
Okay.

KENT
The three of us will get dinner together when you get back.

MATT
Alright.

KENT
Don't be gone too long.

(MATT picks up the plastic bag and exits.)

(KENT watches after him. A beat. KENT moves a lever on the side of the recliner which kicks up the foot rest. He leans back and settles into the chair. A pause. KENT shuts his eyes. KENT opens his eyes.)

(Blackout.)

END

JUNE BRIDE

(Lights up. JENNIFER sits on an old, overstuffed chair near a small telephone table with push-button telephone resting on it. JENNIFER scans through a medium-sized yellow pages. She appears hot and mildly frustrated. A few moments pass as she looks through the phone book, writing down phone numbers on a piece of scrap paper. JENNIFER dials a number on the telephone, listens, then hangs up the receiver.)

(MARY enters. She wears a nice dress suit. MARY stands near JENNIFER, but remains unnoticed. After a beat or two, JENNIFER looks up at MARY. MARY smiles at JENNIFER.

MARY

Aren't you hot?

JENNIFER

It's hot.

MARY

Even though the sun has set, it is so hot. Oh my. It is so hot in here. Have you stayed here before? Is it always so hot in here?

JENNIFER

It's my first time staying here.

MARY

We usually stay at a house in Stillwater but it was full so we decided to stay here. It's sort of like your Aunt's house here, isn't it? It's like you're staying in your Aunt's house with all of the quirks.

JENNIFER

That's true.

MARY

It's like you're staying at your Aunt's house. Do you know how to make the coffee?

JENNIFER

No.

(A beat. JENNIFER dials a number on the telephone. She listens. After a few moments she writes some information down, then hangs up the receiver.)

MARY

There's a coffee pot in that little side room but no one can find the coffee. It's so hot out I don't know why anyone would want some coffee. You don't know how to make it? Do you know where Barb or Michael are? Are they here?

JENNIFER

I actually just got in a few minutes ago, so I'm not sure.

MARY

Don't you think it's strange that neither of them are here, or do they live in the basement? I saw a light on in the basement. This is the strangest bed and breakfast. I can't make coffee and don't you think it is unbearably hot in here?

JENNIFER

My room has air.

MARY

What are you doing? Looking in the yellow pages?

JENNIFER

YES.

MARY

What are you looking in the yellow pages for?

JENNIFER

My car isn't working right.

MARY

Automotive repair?

JENNIFER

Yes.

MARY

What happened to your car? Did it break down?

JENNIFER

No. It's making a strange noise.

MARY

Oh no. Are you on vacation?

JENNIFER

Yes.

MARY

That's really too bad when your car starts acting up on vacation. You're all ready to go then your car breaks down in a strange place then you sit there staring at a yellow pages wondering where to take your car. Did you ask Barb or Michael where you should take your car?

JENNIFER

Not yet.

(JENNIFER dials another number on the telephone. She listens. She writes. She hangs up the receiver.)

MARY

There's probably a neighborhood place. Oh my god it's so hot in here how do you stand it? What is your room going to be like?

JENNIFER

There an air-conditioner in my room.

MARY

I know, but it's probably still a little warm in there.

JENNIFER

It's not.

MARY
Under the covers when you sleep.

JENNIFER
It's not.

MARY
What have you done so far?

JENNIFER
When?

MARY
Here. Where have you visited on your vacation?

JENNIFER
I got into town last night and this morning my car was making a noise so I really haven't done that much.

MARY
Your car is making a noise? What kind of noise is it making?

JENNIFER
Woosh.

MARY
A woosh?

JENNIFER
Woosh woosh woosh.

MARY
Engine belts.

JENNIFER
I'm not sure.

MARY
Where are you from?

JENNIFER
Chicago.

MARY

We're from Peoria.

(MARY exits. A long pause. JENNIFER starts to dial the telephone, then returns it to its cradle. MARY returns.)

MARY (cont'd)

My niece is getting married and everyone is staying at my sister's house except us because they didn't have any room for old people. Like us. Every night one or two of the cousins or grandchildren is going to stay out here with us in one of the other rooms. It'll be like camp for them. It's about ninety-seven degrees in here. (pause) What sorts of things are you planning for your vacation?

JENNIFER

I'm not sure.

MARY

What are your plans?

JENNIFER

I used to live here about six years ago and I'm going to go to some of the places I used to visit.

MARY

Like where?

JENNIFER

I'm not sure. My old neighborhood, I guess.

MARY

Where's that?

JENNIFER

West of Uptown.

MARY

Ooh. Uptown?

JENNIFER

West of Uptown.

MARY
Over the bridge?

JENNIFER
Yes.

MARY
Who are you here with?

JENNIFER
No one.

MARY
Do you want to come to my niece's wedding? Just kidding. You're divorced?

JENNIFER
I look divorced?

MARY
You don't look divorced, but are you divorced?

JENNIFER
Yes.

MARY
And on vacation?

JENNIFER
Yes.

MARY
Are you going to the places you and your former husband used to visit?

JENNIFER
I suppose.

MARY
You haven't been divorced very long?

JENNIFER
Ten months.

MARY

Have you ever been to Tuscany?

JENNIFER

No.

(MARY exits. JENNIFER sits silent, staring after MARY. A few beats. MARY enters, carrying an empty coffee cup.)

MARY

We're flying to Tuscany next week. Tuscany, then Rome. We usually stay with a host family in a sister city, but we're traveling into Rome afterwards and we've been to Tuscany before, but not to parts of Tuscany we're going to this time. I was told not to take any jewelry at all, save any rings I'm wearing, because during any European stops the officials go through your bags and they'll steal any jewelry, even if it's glass or "I'll never tell." This chain I'm wearing right now is, "I'll never tell", but I couldn't even wear this in Rome or they would rip it from my neck and there would go the whole thing and I'd probably hurt my neck, too. Have you been to Europe?

JENNIFER

Yes.

MARY

With your ex-husband?

JENNIFER

Yes.

MARY

Where did you go?

JENNIFER

London.

MARY

When?

JENNIFER

Three years ago.

MARY

What time of year?

JENNIFER

Christmas time.

MARY

I've never been there at Christmas time. Was it very pretty? I read that they have all sorts of decorations and Herrod's is decorated wonderfully with trees and crackers and things. Those popping crackers? You know, you pop them when you pull them? I read that Herrod's makes their own crackers with varying price ranges so that if you want a small toy or a paper hat inside your cracker you can have that, or if you want to have crackers that have gold jewelry or nicer items inside, you can have that, too.

JENNIFER

(pointing at the coffee cup) You figured out the coffee?

MARY

No. (turns the empty cup upside down.) It's empty. I'm just holding it. We're off to the rehearsal dinner tonight, and tomorrow is the wedding. You're very young for having been divorced, but it probably was the best thing to do, wasn't it? Things happen that way these days when young people get married. (pointing at an ad in the yellow pages) Ooh, take your car there. That's a nice, big color ad. They must be very good.

JENNIFER

I'm just trying to find a place that's open Saturdays.

MARY

When are you leaving?

JENNIFER

I'm supposed to be checking out on Sunday.

MARY

Your car may not be fixed until Monday.

JENNIFER

I know.

MARY

My niece is twenty and so I think she may be a little young to get married but she's getting married anyway, but Joe is nice, that's his name, "Joe", which is odd, don't you think? You don't hear of too many people with the name Joe these days, or at least going by the name "Joe" if their name is Joseph. The Gay Pride Parade is this weekend, so watch out for that. When you go wandering around your old neighborhood watch out for the Gay Pride Parade.

(JENNIFER again dials the telephone, listens, writes, and hangs up.)

JENNIFER

I didn't get a divorce because I married too young.

MARY

I was talking about my niece.

JENNIFER

I didn't get a divorce because of that.

MARY

I really was talking about her, not you.

(JENNIFER gets up and exits, leaving the yellow pages sitting on the chair. MARY moves the yellow pages to the table. JENNIFER returns.)

JENNIFER

The side room door is locked.

MARY

I think that someone locked it on accident.

JENNIFER

It must have just happened because you have that coffee cup.

MARY

You don't know how to unlock that side room, do you?

JENNIFER

No.

MARY

Did you want something from inside there?

JENNIFER

Just a glass of water.

(JENNIFER sits again and returns to scanning the yellow pages.)

MARY

You can get water in your room.

JENNIFER

I know.

MARY

Then it's okay. I didn't mean to upset you, I know that you, whatever your circumstances, were married for the right reasons and divorced for equally as right reasons. I was talking about my niece, who is getting married for love or something, I'm not sure, but we all came up for the wedding and all five of my children are here which is some sort of summertime miracle. You should be upstairs where it's nice and cool in your room and worry about your engine's belts tomorrow.

JENNIFER

I don't have a problem with doing this here.

MARY

Just take your car in tomorrow and drop it off and rent a car and throw caution to the wind. You shouldn't visit those places that you used to go to six years ago. They'll be depressing and you'll make yourself sad.

JENNIFER

I want to see those places.

MARY

What places are they? Like a park or one of the lakes or something?

JENNIFER

Yes.

MARY

I was told the lakes are now filled with some sort of Vietnamese weed that's taken over. They look very different now, I'm told.

JENNIFER

Oh.

MARY

The Vietnamese threw their garbage in the lakes and so this weed must have been in their garbage so now the weed is everywhere in the lakes. It's pretty terrible, actually.

JENNIFER

I'll go check it out.

MARY

I should go finish getting ready.

(JENNIFER puts away the yellow pages. A beat.)

MARY (cont'd)

You found a place to get your car fixed? Once when my children were very young, our car broke down in the desert. My husband walked to a gas station and left us in the car and he came back later with some men came in a tow truck and they hauled our car away to get repaired. We were all stuck in a motel in the middle of nowhere. It was very scary. One night a strange man knocked at our door and my son, who was five at the time, ran to the door and opened it. The man attempted to come into our room, but my husband quickly locked the door. We called the front desk and they called the police, but they didn't find the man. We would have stayed somewhere else, but there was only the one motel, so we just waited. Two days later the car was finally fixed so we drove the rest of the way on our trip. Good night.

(MARY exits. JENNIFER sits. A few beats. JENNIFER leans back in her chair and shuts her eyes. Lights fade to black.)

END

THE PONG

(Lights up. 1978. BEUTE and YARDLY sit on the ground playing Pong on small black-and-white television. BEUTE wears a light blue polyester leisure suit and YARDLY wears a velour track suit. The Pong in which they play is projected onto a large screen behind them.)

BEUTE

Shit.

YARDLY

Hold on.

BEUTE

Damnit.

YARDLY

Just goddamn wait--

BEUTE

Goddamn it shit.

YARDLY

Look out awwwwww look out--

BEUTE

Pieceashit--

YARDLY

--aw c'mon--

BEUTE

--hell my customers won't want this pieceashit--

YARDLY

How much they gotta buy for 'em to get one--?

BEUTE

--twenty-five--

YARDLY

Twenty-five really ain't that much to buy--

BEUTE

Yeah but shit--

YARDLY

--ya get a Pong at twenty-five and that's not bad--

BEUTE

--buy twenty-five and get a Pong -- so what.

YARDLY

If you were talking to me I'd order twenty-five for a Pong in two seconds.

BEUTE

Everbody's gonna see the Pong and say bullshit.

YARDLY

They gotsa Pong down at Ducks and they also gotsa Sea Hunt which is damn great -- this thing play that?

BEUTE

It play Sea Hunt?

YARDLY

This thing play that?

BEUTE

No itsa Pong only.

YARDLY

Hold on, let me see, it says here it's got five exciting sports -- tennis, catch, baseball, hoop and handball plus authentic ball spin for more competitive action. How much in dollar signs this Pong cost usually?

BEUTE

I don't goddamn know.

YARDLY

Give it a guesstimate.

BEUTE
Who the hell cares? A hundred bucks?

YARDLY
Shitfire howmany Pongs you got?

BEUTE
None -- if a customer buys twenty-five they get a coupon that they drive over to the mall and pick it up their Pong at Dan's Zeniths and Radios.

YARDLY
All the way down to Dan's? That hardly seems fair for buyin' twenty-five -- you gotta go down to the mall pick up yer own goddamn Pong after you spent the money to win it in the first place?

BEUTE
Yeah, well, don't talk to me, talk to Buddy Mountsier.

YARDLY
Buddy Mountsier's the one that thought this goddamn hunt-and-fetch scheme up? (back to the game) Ooo, look out, gotcha on the ropes.

BEUTE
Stupid-ass Pong.

YARDLY
Seems smart to me, a line hitting a ball with only a T.V. to tell it what to do.

BEUTE
Stupid ass Pong.

YARDLY
Alright, how about you, you offer any alternate suggestions to yer boss as far as other types of customer sales incentives?

BEUTE
Yeah of course.

YARDLY
What sorta shit you come up with?

BEUTE

I said maybe at twenty-five the customer gets one of those Avon T-Rex Bubblebaths.

YARDLY

--Avon T-Rex Bubblebath--?

BEUTE

Yeah, the Avon goddamn T-Rex Bubblebath and not the goddamn long-necked asshole-looking Brontosaurus Bubblebath, but the goddamnT-Rex Bubblebath.

YARDLY

Avon T-rex Bubblebath really ain't no Pong.

BEUTE

It's a goddamn T-Rex!

YARDLY

Yeah, but don'tcha think a T-Rex reminds everybody of the extinct past and not of what's comin' up? You wanna remind everybody of the future, don'tcha instead?

BEUTE

I suppose.

YARDLY

What Buddy Mountsier say about yer T-Rex Bubblebath suggestion?

BEUTE

I don't remember but I remember I says to Buddy Mountsier how about instead of the T-Rex bubblebath, instead we do like a whole Avon gift set thing?

YARDLY

You know what I think? I think you only suggesting Avon cuz Jean sells Avon.

BEUTE

Hell I am. My Avon suggestions got nothin' to do with Jean.

YARDLY
I see those dollar signs in yer eyes.

BEUTE
Shutup.

YARDLY
Avon shit means money money money.

BEUTE
(stands, suddenly in a rage) Fuck you I'll mess you up with this Pong!

YARDLY
--aw--

BEUTE
I'll hit you with the goddamn Pong set ya don't shutup about me and Avon!

YARDLY
--calm it down--

BEUTE
(a beat) (sits back down) That's what I thought.

YARDLY
I gotta admit, though, Avon do got a nice man page in their catalog.

BEUTE
Yeah, Avon's got a good man page for sure.

YARDLY
I saw on that man page once they had a aftershave in the shape of the goddamn Liberty Bell.

BEUTE
Those brush/combs that fits in yer hand are damn nice, too.

YARDLY
So you get to keep this Pong as a for instance?

BEUTE
I suppose.

YARDLY

Man, this Pong is like playing tennis or catch or hoop or handball or baseball for real.

BEUTE

Shit it is not.

YARDLY

Maybe you're right, but I bet in the future, though, I bet someday people won't be able to tell the difference between real sports and T.V. Pong sports. Everybody will do stuff and play sports like they was a glowing stick that can only move up and down until some glowing ball comes by and ya hit it with your face, just hopin' your opponent down the other side misses so you can go about your life without having to use your face to hit that goddamn glowing ball again.

BEUTE

Sounds like a shitty typea future to me.

YARDLY

Sounds sorta like a strange kinda heaven to me. A strange kinda heaven on some dark and sacred earth.

(BEUTE and YARDLY play pong. Lights fade.)

END

STATIC NICE BY HELEN K. YEER

(Lights up. Four chairs sit in a half circle. Four women, CHERYL, SUSAN, JILL and JENNY, sit in the chairs. Each has the same book, *Static Nice by Helen K. Yeer*. Some have a notebook, some have coffee. They sit silently for a moment.)

CHERYL

Where's the restroom?

JILL

Past the counter. (Points.)

(CHERYL leaves her book on her chair and exits.)

(Long pause.)

SUSAN

This is a nice Starbucks.

JILL

It's new.

JENNY

They were building one about a block from me, and they stopped. It's still sitting empty.

JILL

A Starbucks?

JENNY

Yes.

JILL

They don't stop building Starbucks.

JENNY

It's a Starbucks.

JILL

Did it have a sign for Starbucks on the outside?

JENNY
No.

JILL
What did it look like inside?

JENNY
The windows are all boarded up, so I only saw the inside once. The workers were loading in a counter when I was walking by.

JILL
It looked like a Starbucks inside?

JENNY
Yes.

JILL
They wouldn't wait to open a Starbucks.

JENNY
I thought it was a Starbucks.

SUSAN
Sometimes their coffee gives me a headache.

JILL
It's too strong.

JENNY
Sometimes.

JILL
It burns my throat.

SUSAN
Did you guys like the book?

JENNY
It was good.

JILL
We shouldn't talk about the book until everyone's here.

(A pause.)

JILL (cont'd)
Did you guys have your client services meeting last week?

SUSAN
Yes.

JILL
Did they tell you that you'd be training for sales?

SUSAN
Yeah.

JILL
Sales isn't part of my job.

JENNY
I know. I don't want to do sales.

SUSAN
I don't want to have to re-learn everything, then learn pricing.

JILL
I talked to Kathy and told her that I felt very strongly that I couldn't do sales at all.

SUSAN
I have to train next week.

JILL
Tell them you don't want to.

SUSAN
It's scheduled.

JILL
Tell them that it's not part of your job. I'm going to talk to Mark and tell him that I was hired for creative, and they need to either hire more people for sales, or train the people they have better. They're just pushing this entire work load over on us, and there's nothing we can do but end up doing all the work. Their answer is always to give our departments more of the work so that the other departments can take it slow. It's unfair and idiotic.

JENNY

When are you talking to Mark?

JILL

Next week. We should all go in there together and tell him that we're not going to do sales.

SUSAN

When next week?

JILL

I'm off Monday, so probably Wednesday or Thursday.

SUSAN

I start training on Monday.

JILL

You should talk to him on Monday, then.

SUSAN

I'm not talking to Mark by myself.

JILL

You and Jenny could go.

JENNY

(to SUSAN) If you train on Monday, I probably do, too.

SUSAN

I think you probably do.

JILL

That doesn't mean that we can't talk to Mark after you train.

SUSAN

We've already started training then.

JILL

I'll talk to Kathy first, and see what she says. You guys should talk to Sydney and tell her that you don't want to train for sales.

SUSAN
I'm in training all day on Monday, and Jenny probably is, too.

JILL
It doesn't seem right that we have to have sales training while the sales people all sit around, logging off and sending calls over to us. I've seem Alan Harlin logged off almost every time I pass his desk. He just sits there and plays on his computer. They should be supervising their sales staff much better if they want better sales. We're doing our part already.

SUSAN
There must have been a line at the bathroom.

JENNY
I think they only have one bathroom here.

JILL
A unisex bathroom?

JENNY
Right.

JILL
Whenever I go into a unisex bathroom it's disgusting.

SUSAN
They have a unisex bathroom at Starbucks?

JENNY
I thought so.

SUSAN
I think they're required to have women's and men's bathrooms.

JENNY
I thought for some reason there was only one at this Starbucks.

JILL
I went into a unisex bathroom one time and there was a man masturbating in the stall.

SUSAN
What?

JENNY

Where was this?

JILL

It was at a bookstore. I was waiting for the bathroom, and I knocked and no one answered, so I opened the door. There was a stall, and the door was shut. I saw his hairy legs and he was wearing Teva shoes.

JENNY

What are Teva shoes?

JILL

Those rubber sandals.

JENNY

What do they look like?

JILL

They're brown and black and they have Velcro straps over the top.

JENNY

A rubber sandal?

JILL

Right.

JENNY

I've seen those. They make your feet look huge.

SUSAN

I used to have a pair of those.

JENNY

They make your feet look huge.

SUSAN

I think it's because of the rubber sole. It sticks out at the top and makes your toes look long.

JENNY

Why would you buy those?

SUSAN

They were comfortable.

(A pause.)

JILL
He was making masturbating sounds, too.

SUSAN
Yuck!

JENNY
He probably had a book from the bookstore and the book was about erotica or something.

JILL
Probably.

SUSAN
Then he put it back on the shelf.

JENNY
Eww!

(SUSAN and JENNY laugh.)

SUSAN
Which bookstore was it?

JILL
Bachbrothers.

SUSAN
Where is that?

JILL
In Minneapolis.

SUSAN
Were you living there?

JILL
No.

(A pause.)

SUSAN
Maybe we should go see if Cheryl is all right.

JENNY
Maybe she's been hypnotized by a masterbator!

(SUSAN and JENNY laugh.)

SUSAN
Maybe she's not feeling well.

JILL
She's probably getting something to eat.

SUSAN
I'll go check on her.

(SUSAN exits.)

(A pause.)

JENNY
Who else is coming?

JILL
Lisa might come and Penny Yardly might be here. I talked to her on Friday and sent her an e-mail telling her where we were.

JENNY
Did she read the book?

JILL
She knew what book we were reading.

JENNY
You told her on Friday?

JILL
I e-mailed her the list a month ago, so she knew what book we'd be discussing.

JENNY
She should be here by now, don't you think?

JILL

Probably.

JENNY

It might just be the four of us.

JILL

Maybe.

JENNY

That'd be okay. It's easier to talk when there's less people.

JILL

Sometimes.

JENNY

I'm really looking forward to talking about this book. I liked it a lot.

JILL

As soon as Cheryl and Susan come back, we'll start.

JENNY

I really liked the part when the two women are out in the desert, and they're walking.

JILL

I don't want to talk about the book yet.

JENNY

I'm not really talking about the book.

JILL

I want to make sure that the things we talk about are fresh, and if we start talking about them when everyone's not here, then we'll lose perspective into what we're talking about. It's best to not pre-think anything when we're talking about the book.

JENNY

Okay.

JILL
I've been researching the best way talk about whatever we're reading, and they make a strong point to not talk about the book until everyone can hear what everyone in the group's individual reactions are.

JENNY
I'll save what I said until they come back.

JILL
That's not really what I mean.

JENNY
I'll talk about other things, too. I'll talk about both.

JILL
You weren't here last time.

JENNY
I couldn't make it last time.

JILL
It was a good book. Did you read the book?

JENNY
Yes.

JILL
We had a great discussion.

JENNY
Who showed up?

JILL
Susan, Lisa, Cheryl and I. We met at a different place, over near Lisa's.

JENNY
Oh.

JILL
I was thinking next time we should try and meet at places that relate to the book. Like this week, it would have been nice to meet at an old diner.

JENNY
That would have been a great idea.

JILL

Then we could have talked about what it would have been like to work in a diner, and we could imagine the world of the book better.

JENNY

When the sister was working in the diner, it felt so real. The descriptions were very realistic.

JILL

That's why it would have been nice to be at a diner.

JENNY

That is a real good idea. We should do that next time.

JILL

Okay.

JENNY

I like that idea.

JILL

Okay. I'll see what to do.

JENNY

Okay.

JILL

I was thinking that it would have been fun to be at a German coffee house last time, but I don't know where any of them are.

JENNY

I don't know where there are any German coffee houses either.

(SUSAN enters. She has a coffee.)

SUSAN

I think she's still in there. I think there was a line.

JENNY

What did you get?

SUSAN

A "coffee of the day".

JENNY

What kind is it?

SUSAN

I don't know. It tastes like hazelnut.

JENNY

Sometimes they have three or four "coffees of the day".

SUSAN

At Starbucks?

JENNY

Sometimes.

SUSAN

I usually just get the coffee of the day.

JILL

Cheryl is in the bathroom now?

SUSAN

I think so. The door's shut and I didn't see her.

JILL

I thought maybe Lisa and Penny Yardly might be coming, but we can get started without them.

SUSAN

Penny Yardly might come?

JILL

She said she might be here.

SUSAN

When did you talk to her?

JILL

I sent her an e-mail.

SUSAN

What did she say?

JILL

She didn't tell me if she was coming or not, but I talked to her about a week ago and she said she might come.

SUSAN

She was out sick on Friday, I think.

JILL

She was?

SUSAN

I think.

JILL

I don't think Lisa's going to make it, so it's probably just the four of us.

JENNY

I hope Cheryl's not sick.

SUSAN

She probably just got in there.

JILL

I was telling Jenny that maybe we should start meeting at places that relate to the book.

SUSAN

That's a good idea.

JILL

Like this week, it would have been great to meet in an old diner.

SUSAN

That would have been great.

JILL

We could have felt like we were in the world of the book.

SUSAN

That's a good idea. We should do that next time.

JILL

I'll have to think about where we can go.

JENNY

What book is next week?

JILL

It's "Snip Pah Boys" by Theresa Villa.

SUSAN

Who's book is that?

JILL

It was Cheryl's pick.

SUSAN

What's it about?

JILL

I don't want to ruin it for you. After you read it, it'll be obvious where we'll meet. I just have to find the best one of those kinds of places for us.

SUSAN

Okay.

JENNY

It's a good idea.

JILL

I found out about doing that sort of thing when I was doing my research.

SUSAN

Are we waiting for Lisa?

JILL

No. If she shows up, we can go from there.

SUSAN

Okay.

(CHERYL enters.)

CHERYL

Sorry I was gone so long.

JILL

That's okay.

SUSAN

Are you okay?

CHERYL

I had to go out to my car and I ran into a friend of mine from high school.

JENNY

Just now?

CHERYL

It was so weird.

JENNY

Who was it?

CHERYL

This girl I knew from high school.

JENNY

That's great.

CHERYL

She wants to go get some lunch, and I haven't seen her in a really long time, so if it's okay, I'm going to go to lunch with her. I don't mean to mess this all up.

JILL

It's okay.

CHERYL

I really want to talk about this book, though. I really liked it a lot.

SUSAN

So did I.

JENNY

So did I.

CHERYL
If it's at all possible, can we switch this to next Sunday? I really want to talk about this book.

JENNY
Next Sunday?

SUSAN
That's fine with me.

JENNY
Okay.

JILL
Next Sunday is okay.

CHERYL
I don't mean to mess this whole thing up.

JILL
It's okay. Lisa and Penny Yardly aren't here yet, so maybe next week is better.

SUSAN
Actually, next week would be better for me anyhow.

JILL
Okay.

JENNY
We can do the diner thing then.

CHERYL
What diner thing?

JENNY
Jill thought we could meet at a diner like in the book.

CHERYL
That's a great idea.

SUSAN
Yeah.

CHERYL
Okay. Well, thanks. I'll see you on Monday, then we'll do this next Sunday. Sorry.

JILL
That's okay.

CHERYL
Bye!

JENNY
Bye.

SUSAN
See you!

JILL
Bye.

(CHERYL exits. A pause.)

JILL (cont'd)
Next Sunday's okay with everybody?

SUSAN
Yeah.

JENNY
I'll check, but I'm sure it's okay.

JILL
Okay. Next week it'll still be "Static Nice".

JENNY
Okay.

SUSAN
I should go run some errands. Jenny, do you need a ride?

JENNY
Sure. Thanks.

SUSAN
Okay. See you, Jill.

JENNY

See you Monday.

JILL

See you Monday.

SUSAN

Bye.

JENNY

Bye.

(SUSAN and JENNY exit with their books, SUSAN with her coffee.)

(A few beats.)

(JILL sits and thumbs through her book.)

(Lights fade to black.)

END

THE AUDIT

(Lights up. In the center of the room is a table piled with stacks of papers and yellow legal pads. A large coffee cup rests on the table. At the table are three chairs, two chairs placed each other and another that faces the piles of paperwork and yellow legal pads. A pause.)

(DON enters. He wears an open collar shirt, khaki pants and nice shoes. He is followed by DANA and BETH, both wearing semi-dress casual attire.)

DON

Do either of you want some coffee?

DANA

Your coffee is so strong! (laughs)

DON

(laughs) Yeah, you know but that's the way I like it and, well, around tax time it's good and strong so I guess it just ends up being strong all the time so I'm used to it that way all the time, it's strong stuff, yeah. (laughs)

DANA

It is, you're right.

DON

So, yeah.

DANA

I'll have some, though.

DON

Sounds good! Does Beth want some coffee?

DANA

(to BETH) Do you want some coffee? Yes?

BETH

Yes.

DON

Do either of you take anything in your coffee?

DANA

Some Equal?

DON

Equal. Beth?

BETH

No.

DON

No?

BETH

No Equal.

DON

No Equal?

BETH

No.

DON

Just nothing?

BETH

Yes.

(DON exits.)

(BETH and DANA sit in the two chairs near each other. A long pause.)

(DON enters with two small coffee cups on saucers. The Equal packet rests on DANA's saucer.)

DON

Here you go.

(DON hands the cups of coffee to DANA and BETH.)

DANA

Aw, thanks, sheesh.

DON

I put the Equal there on the side.

DANA

Wonderful.

DON

And find some room to put the coffee down there on the table if you can, sorry, sorry about the mess, sorry, sorry, eek.

DANA

No, it's all right, we understand, you're busy.

DON

You wouldn't believe, it's so strange, I'm so busy, this time of year I'm not usually that busy but this year, oh my god I'm really just tied up, look at all this.

DANA

It doesn't usually look like this in here, really.

DON

Well, this year, I don't know, this year, the economy--

DANA

Oh yes, the economy, I'm sure, everybody--

DON

Everything, you know, it's sort of crazy and so it's busy as a result.

DANA

It really looks like it.

DON

So try to make some room on the table there for your coffee if you can, just move some things, throw stuff on the floor if you want, hell, take some of it home, put it in your bag and take some of it home, that would be great! (laughs)

DANA

No thank you. (laughs)

DON

No, no, take it, get it out of here! (laughs)

DANA

No, no thanks, no thank you.

DON

(to BETH) Hell, Beth, you take it.

BETH

No.

DON

Just take it, take it all! (laughs) I could use the help, I'm drowning in paperwork!

BETH

It looks like it.

DON

I am. I am drowning in paperwork. (pause) Hey. So. I met with them, as I told you on the phone, I met with them, and thanks for coming down to go over this in person, there are a number of remaining questions they had, like I said, as I expected and we can go over some things, does that sound okay?

DANA

Sure.

DON

Okay.

DANA

It sounds okay, sure.

DON

There were a few questions but not anything that you should really get alarmed or worried really about.

DANA

Good.

DON

Those auditing teams down there can sometimes be a little feisty, but they were fine, they were fine when I was there and actually I knew one of the four in the team from a previous audit I had a few months ago, you wouldn't believe, I've had <u>four</u> audits I've gone through with other clients in the past three months, did I mention that before? But knowing that person, that woman on your team when I was there certainly helped but of course there are some questions that came up, there are questions, but, anyway, I can ask you both now and then I'll go back to the team with your answers, does that sound good?

DANA

You have to go back?

DON

Oh, it's nothing, no, no, it's nothing, but I do have to go back and meet with them again, they want me to come back after I talk to you, after I ask you about a few other things, they want me to come back, I'll call them and get a date from them and I'll go back down there on that date they give me after I talk to both of you, after I see what sort of things we can come up with here, okay?

DANA

What else did they need to know?

DON

Nothing huge.

DANA

Good.

DON

They had questions on a few receipts, that's all, they just wanted to get a little more "in depth" on a few items.

DANA

Oh.

DON

Just "in depth" on a few things.

DANA

No problem.

DON

Okay.

DANA

No problem.

DON

So. Aw. Hold on, just a sec, I'll be right back, I need to go get your stuff, it's over in the file area, okay? Does anybody want any water or anything?

DANA

No thanks.

BETH

Yes.

DON

Beth? Water?

BETH

Yes.

DON

Do you take anything in your water? (laughs)

BETH

No.

DON

Nothing? That would be weird if you did take something "in your water", wouldn't it? So. I'll be right back.

(DON exits. A beat.)

(DON returns quickly with a glass of water. He hands the glass of water to BETH.)

DON (cont'd)

Here you go and let me go get your stuff I just wanted to get your water first I'll be right back.

(DON exits.)

BETH

(whispering) Oh no!

DANA

(whispering) Shut-up!

BETH

Oh no oh no oh no oh no!

DANA

Shut-up!

BETH

Oh no!

DANA

Beth!

BETH

Ug!

DANA

Shut-up!

BETH

Ug!

DANA

Shut-up!

BETH

Ug!

DANA

Shut-up!

BETH

Ug!

(DON enters with a cardboard box.)

DON

Ooo! My back! Heavy! (laughs, slumps a bit)

(DON sits, putting the box on the floor near his feet.)

DON (cont'd)

Okay. Let's see.

(DON opens the box and pulls a number of files out.)

DON (cont'd)

What I wanted to do, what they had questions about were with some of your receipts like I said, some of the origins of the receipts for your business.

DANA

Okay.

DON

The receipts total to a rather large amount--

DANA

Not that large, really.

DON

Well, when we did this before, when we went over this before, everything, it sounded all fine to me but when I met with the audit people, that's when questions came up.

DANA

Okay.

DON

Good.

DANA

What questions did they have?

(DON opens one of the folders.)

DON

Okay. Let me see here. Let me find... Let me find what they were asking about.

(DON looks through the folder, then through the other. He pulls a few other folders from the box and shuffles through those. He finds a pile of odd shaped receipts.)

DON (cont'd)

Here we go, here we go, this should be it, here we go.

(DON sips his coffee.)

DON (cont'd)

Wow! Strong like you said, I make it so strong! Look out! (pause) Okay. Hm.

(DON looks over the receipts.)

DANA

Which did they have questions--

DON

Hold on, hold on.

(A pause. DON shuffles through the stack. He pulls out a receipt.)

DON (cont'd)

Okay. Well. Okay. This one? This one here?

(DON looks at the receipt for a moment, then holds it out to DANA. DANA takes the receipt.)

DANA

Oh. Yes.

DON

What is that purchase?

DANA

It says what the purchase is here on the receipt.

DON

Yes, well, yeah. But what is it?

DANA
It's a receipt for "Mr. Purple".

DON
Yes, what, though, sorry, this is for me to let them know because they had a question about that receipt, they wanted to know what exactly is "Mr. Purple"?

DANA
It should be obvious from the distributor's name, don't you think?

DON
Yes, yes, that's probably true, but in order to clarify for the audit team, what exactly is "Mr. Purple"?

DANA
A… Sexual aide.

DON
A sexual aide of which style?

DANA
Which style?

DON
Yes.

DANA
A sexual aide as the store name implies.

DON
What is the store name, and again, this is just getting to matters I need to clarify because it is me there in the room representing you both and these questions have come up, so what is the store name if that helps define what exactly it is that "Mr. Purple" is?

DANA
"Mr. Purple" is a dildo.

DON
Yes.

DANA

Which should be implied because the distributor's name is called "The Dildo Store".

DON

Right. "The Dildo Store". Yes.

DANA

That's where this specific dildo was purchased.

DON

Which is stated on the receipt.

DANA

Yes.

DON

"The Dildo Store".

DANA

Yes.

DON

"The Dildo Store", Lexington, Kentucky?

DANA

It was an "internet purchase".

DON

Right.

DANA

That is an "internet receipt".

DON

I see, yes.

DANA

I know, though, it is a bit e-mail-y looking but that is the only document they sent as a receipt and we needed to purchase an item like that item for business use.

DON

Yes, yes, of course.

DANA

So, it's a legitimate business expense, I don't understand the misgivings.

DON

Yes.

DANA

It was a business expense.

DON

Okay. Right. I understand. I guess what I need to know, and I understand the internet and how things work, e-mail receipts, but I did a little research, only due to questions asked of me by the audit team and I couldn't find a store called "The Dildo Store" in Lexington, Kentucky.

DANA

Well, maybe they have closed, I'm not sure.

DON

Do you purchase items such as that item often?

DANA

Yes. All the time. We buy those all the time, every week.

DON

But not from "The Dildo Store" any longer?

DANA

No, not since they may have closed.

DON

But you don't know if they have closed?

DANA

I don't know if they're closed or not, but we don't buy things from them--

DON

"The Dildo Store"?

DANA

--yes, “The Dildo Store”, we don’t buy things from them any longer, we had a dispute with them in the past and so we said we were buying from someone else now and so that’s what we’re doing, we don’t buy any dildos from them anymore, no.

DON

Okay. Fair enough. Good.

DANA

Yes.

DON

Okay. Let’s see.

(DON shuffles through the receipts.)

DON (CONT’D)

Oh yes. Okay. This one, this one here, wait, wait, is it a little warmish in here? They’re working on the ducts in the building so the air isn’t circulating right so, are either of you warm in here at all?

DANA

I’m fine.

DON

It’s a little stuffy, I’m a little upset about the building doing the duct work today but I’m probably the only one here toiling away on a Saturday morning and thanks for making it down on a Saturday, I know how sometimes that’s hard.

DANA

It’s no problem.

DON

Do you both have plans then, this weekend? What are you up to?

(A pause.)

DANA

We have our sex-show. (pause) We have our sex-show to do this afternoon. And then another of our sex-shows tonight. And then tomorrow we have, oh, three or four sex-shows tomorrow.

DON

I'm going to a cookout.

DANA

Oh yes?

DON

I'm going to a cookout at my sister's house. It should be very fun. Maybe we'll toss a frisbee around, I hope we toss a frisbee. (pause) Right, yes. (pause) This other receipt?

(DON hands DANA a very, very long receipt.)

DANA

It's a very long receipt, isn't it?

DON

Yes.

DANA

A big purchase, then.

DON

Yes. Everything looks fine, though, as far as it being a business receipt. So. That was are…?

DANA

Yes?

DON

Those items are for exactly…?

DANA

Our sex-show. It's a business receipt, as you stated.

DON

Yes.

DANA
Things for the show.

DON
Such as? What does it say there?

DANA
Well, it looks like we bought some, um, "pork chops".

DON
All right.

DANA
And then we bought some "Cheerios".

DON
Yes.

DANA
And then we bought some "Rolaids".

DON
Yes.

DANA
All, definitely, yes, all for Beth and my sexy sex-show that we perform.

DON
Yes.

(A pause. DON pulls a large folder out of the box.)

DON (CONT'D)
There were also a few questions about a number of other things.

DANA
There are?

DON
Yes.

DANA
How many?

DON

How many questions?

DANA

Yes.

DON

There a just a number of questions, that's all. Just a few. Just a number.

DANA

That's a big folder.

DON

There are just a few more questions they had, that's all.

DANA

That's a very big folder. What's in that folder, what are you asking about?

DON

Let me open it.

DANA

Okay.

DON

Here, I'm opening it.

(DON opens the folder. He looks over a few papers.)

DON

Just… It's just… Well, the questions in this folder concern the car you both drive.

DANA

You mean the car where we "fuck"?

DON

"Fuck"?

DANA

Yes, that's the dirty way of saying "sex" and I've decided that since that's how we all say "sex" in the sex-show business I'm going to say "fuck" for a while instead of "sex", for business reasons, if that's all right with you, I'm going to say "fuck" instead of "sex" while we speak.

DON

If you think that may help, that's no problem, sure.

DANA

Then. "Fuck".

DON

So you have sex in the car.

DANA

We "fuck" in the car.

DON

The audit team had questions--

DANA

We "fuck" right there in our car.

DON

Yes.

DANA

If you can explain that to them. Beth and I "fuck" in the car, that's our sex-show.

DON

I did explain that to them.

DANA

Were they too embarrassed, were they too much of uptight suit-wearing uptight men to believe "fucking" like that, "fucking" in a car -- and I mean two sisters "fucking" in a car for a wild sex-show, did they think, did they think, "Holy-moly, hey! That is way too much to handle?" Is that what they were thinking?

DON

No, no. No. It's not that. No. It's just that your receipts, they were saying, not me, the audit team was saying that your receipts don't seem to support this business, your expenses seem, well, the word they used is, um, "vague".

DANA

"Vague"?

DON

Yes.

DANA

None of it is very "vague" at all.

DON

Right.

DANA

The car is a legitimate expense.

DON

Yes.

DANA

The grocery items are for sexy -- er -- fuck-like purposes.

DON

I understand.

DANA

And the dildo, I mean, come on, it's a dildo.

DON

Right.

DANA

And we've been doing this a long time, Beth and I, a very long time, our "Sex Show In A Car Extravaganza", our sister sex act show extravaganza for a few years now and there's never been a question in the past.

DON

Right, yes. But now there is.

DANA

Well, it's true. It is a business.

DON

Yes.

DANA

Is there some sort of proof you need?

DON

No.

DANA

Because we can provide proof.

DON

No, no.

DANA

We can prove to you our sex-show, that is no problem.

DON

That is okay.

DANA

No, no, here, here, we'll prove it.

DON

You don't need to.

DANA

We don't have a car here, but we will, here, we will do something, here wait, you'll see this and it will be sexy, so, come on Beth, come on. Let's do this, come on.

BETH

What?

DANA

A bit of our sex-show.

BETH

No.

DANA

Clothes on, though, not the nude sex-show, okay?

BETH

No.

DANA

Yes.

BETH

No.

(DANA pulls BETH out of her chair and moves her around, taking stiff and odd liberties with the space around BETH. BETH is confused and embarrassed and struggles with DANA.)

DANA

We usually start with some crazy stuff like we do a strip-tease and then we just get to it, we move our hips around and then one of us jumps up and down and after that then the fucking takes place, two sisters having sex, it blows your mind, and in a car no less and with Mr. Purple in and out of things and then with pork chops over here or something and then there are Cheerios all over this way and then the big topper are the Rolaids all sexy all over the place oh my god oh my god. But, yeah. It's hard to… You get the point, you see where this is going? Right? You see this?

DON

Sure.

(DANA lets go of BETH. BETH slides into her chair. A beat.)

DANA

So there you go.

DON

It makes sense, yes.

DANA

Good.

DON

Yes.

DANA

So there you go.

DON

Right.

(A pause.)

BETH

Um. (pause) (to DON) Do you have any children? What's your hometown? Where did you park your car? Have you ever been to the ocean? Have you ever owned a cat? What do you think of gourmet hot-dogs? Have you ever been to the Grand Canyon? What did you have for breakfast? Where did you go to college? When was the last time you ate at taco salad? What is your favorite book? What region are your ancestors from? Do you prefer red or white wine? Do you read novels? Are you eating enough protein? Did you ever lose your wallet? Do you like to dance? Did you call your mother? Have you waterskied before? Is this the best way to use chopsticks? Is that the last of the coleslaw? Is it cold outside? Has it started? Is it finished? What's the score? Need a hand? Need a lift? Can I get you another glass of soda? Where are my earmuffs?

(A pause.)

DON

You'll both be getting a letter.

DANA

We will?

DON

From the Department of Treasury.

DANA

Yes.

DON

And so. That's it, I guess.

DANA

All right.

DON

So. (pause) That coffee of mine is giving me a little acid reflux. (pause) Well. So. Goodbye.

DANA

Yes, well. Bye.

(DANA exits.)

(DON and BETH stare at each other.)

(BETH exits.)

(A beat.)

(DON sips his coffee.)

(Blackout.)

END

THE NORELCO

(Lights up on a basement. It is 1978. SCOTT and MYER sit on a couch. A large console television rests nearby. A football game plays on the console television.)

SCOTT

Thirty blades.

MYER

Individual?

SCOTT

Yeah, and "no gotcha."

MYER

You gotta clean it, though?

SCOTT

Cleanin's a snap.

MYER

A snap?

SCOTT

You pop the thing, the blades come out, the things pop out, you gotta little brush and you move it around then stuff comes out then you pop the whole thing back and done.

MYER

Every time?

SCOTT

Not every time.

MYER

Every other time?

SCOTT

Maybe, so what?

MYER
All that poppin', what happens you lose a piece?

SCOTT
I'm not losing a piece.

MYER
Not "you," but the general "you."

SCOTT
The royal "you?"

MYER
What if you lose a piece, you gotta replace it?

SCOTT
You gotta replace pieces in the other one anyhow.

MYER
What pieces?

SCOTT
You gotta replace blades.

MYER
I been usin' Bics.

SCOTT
Freakin' waste!

MYER
Good for the wallet.

SCOTT
The Norelco's good for the wallet, saving me time every day.

MYER
What, more time for coffee with Bev is timed saved?

SCOTT
It is.

MYER

Sounds like some damn special moments are happenin' for you, la tah tah tah.

SCOTT

You go on ahead and instead how about me, I'll go and shave like a man.

MYER

I shave like a man already.

SCOTT

You're wrong.

MYER

I'm not wrong.

SCOTT

I'm a man. Norelco's the best.

MYER

I like my Barbasol, my Bic, my warm water in the sink. It's like I'm painting or laying a brick wall on my face.

(A beat.)

SCOTT

That's disgusting.

MYER

It's not either.

SCOTT

I'm gonna toss chunks.

MYER

All I'm saying is it's like I get up outa bed and give myself a morning rubdown for my mind.

(A pause.)

SCOTT

You know what? Forget it. Just -- eat my dust.

(SCOTT and MYER watch the television for awhile.)

MYER

Go Bears.

SCOTT

Yeah. Sure. Go goddamn Bears.

(A pause. Lights fade to black.)

END

WIGWAM

(Lights up on a small motel bed, a motel chair and a few suitcases. Seated on the bed is MATTHEW. MATTHEW wears a short-sleeved button up shirt, slacks, a cheap-looking Native American headdress and his faced is dashed with broad strokes of poorly applied "war paint." Seated on the chair is LAWRENCE. LAWRENCE wears jeans, a bolo tie and a long sleeve shirt. A pause)

LAWRENCE

Eh --

MATTHEW

No.

LAWRENCE

How about --

MATTHEW

No --

LAWRENCE

Maybe a swim?

MATTHEW

This is what we're doing.

LAWRENCE

You bring your swim suit?

MATTHEW

No.

LAWRENCE

Well shoot.

(A long pause.)

MATTHEW
I bet we can't even take the ashtrays anymore.

LAWRENCE
There's no ashtrays --

MATTHEW
That's my point --

LAWRENCE
"No smoking."

MATTHEW
We could have taken an ashtray. As a souvenir. And other things, anything with the wigwam name or wigwam logo, they encouraged you take.

LAWRENCE
There's a big "no smoking" sign by the door.

MATTHEW
You're not hearing me --

LAWRENCE
I doubt they would have wanted you to take stuff.

MATTHEW
They did want it.

LAWRENCE
Maybe in, like, nineteen fifty-six --

MATTHEW
Nineteen fifty-six?

LAWRENCE
You can't go back in time.

(A pause.)

MATTHEW
Is that a dig?

LAWRENCE
A dig?

MATTHEW
Yes.

LAWRENCE
A dig at what?

MATTHEW
This.

LAWRENCE
What?

MATTHEW
This thing --

LAWRENCE
No --

MATTHEW
You have to make a dig.

LAWRENCE
I was only reacting. To what you said. About stealing.

MATTHEW
It wouldn't have been stealing! They wanted you to take that stuff! It was an honest to god marketing thing!!!

LAWRENCE
Are you gonna shout at me this whole visit? 'Cause these damn rooms echo like a sumabitch, with all the concrete and stucco --

MATTHEW
Another dig

LAWRENCE
Everything's not about you.

MATTHEW
Actually, this visit, it *is* about me. Every bit of it All we do, say, touch and speak, it's all about me.

LAWRENCE
I'm screwed, then, naturally.

MATTHEW
Wonderful, wonderful, nice talk.

LAWRENCE
I think maybe your real reason you wanted to visit and stay in these weird-smelling "wigwams" --

MATTHEW
They do not smell weird --

LAWRENCE
-- was to hole me up in here and yell at me for two goddamn days.

MATTHEW
Wow.

LAWRENCE
And that's no good for me.

MATTHEW
Complain if you've got the balls.

(A pause.)

LAWRENCE
I've got no complaints.

MATTHEW
Smelly room. That was a complaint.

LAWRENCE
I take it back.

MATTHEW
You know what this is.

LAWRENCE
I guess --

MATTHEW
You only have to sit there.

LAWRENCE
Oh joy.

(A pause.)

MATTHEW
Maybe unpack your suitcase.

LAWRENCE
Unpack it?

MATTHEW
Unpack your suitcase.

LAWRENCE
We're not gonna be here long enough for me to unpack it.

MATTHEW
Unpack.

LAWRENCE
How about I pretend to unpack?

(A pause.)

MATTHEW
All right.

(LAWRENCE crosses to one of the suitcases. He picks it up and puts it on the bed. A pause. LAWRENCE begins to badly pantomime unpacking the suitcase. A pause.)

MATTHEW
Can you at least unzip it?

LAWRENCE
But I'm nearly through "unpacking."

(A beat. LAWRENCE unzips the suitcase.)

MATTHEW
In my mind, "ziiiip" -- that was the sound I would have heard.

LAWRENCE
You weren't here --

MATTHEW
I should have been.

LAWRENCE
It wasn't on purpose --

MATTHEW
I undoubtably should have been here --

LAWRENCE
I didn't mean to stay here to begin with, it wasn't planned.

(MATTHEW removes a postcard from his pants pocket.)

MATTHEW
(reading from the back) "Staying at this place along Route 66! All the rooms are giant wigwams! Wish you were here! Love, Dad!" (puts the postcard back in his pocket) (long pause) Tell me a campfire story.

LAWRENCE
No.

MATTHEW
Play me a beat on a deerskin drum.

LAWRENCE
No.

MATTHEW
Shoot a bow and arrow in the air.

LAWRENCE
No.

MATTHEW
Poke a stick through the skin on my chest and make me go through some sort of horrible and painful test that will allow me to go from boy to man.

(A beat.)

LAWRENCE

No.

MATTHEW

You took all the fun.

LAWRENCE

I didn't.

MATTHEW

You could have stayed anyplace else.

LAWRENCE

I couldn't have.

MATTHEW

You taunted me.

LAWRENCE

I didn't.

MATTHEW

I was six years old and you taunted me with your fun.

LAWRENCE

Far from it.

MATTHEW

You loved the wigwam motel. You thought it was....spectacular.

(A pause. LAWRENCE exits. A pause. LAWRENCE returns with a plastic motel trash can. He sits in the chair and turns the trash can over. He begins a beat. He begins an "Indian chant." After a few times through, MATTHEW slowly joins him. The two men get rather wild with the drumming and the chanting until they poop out. A pause.)

LAWRENCE

That, the thing...what we just did, plus the stuff on your head, this motel, maybe even the word "wigwam," I think, especially since here they look more like "tee-pees," another word I'm sure is a generalization, it's all, it's all probably all really, really offensive to the native culture of this area.

(A pause. MATTHEW removes his headdress.)

MATTHEW

Now I feel like a total asshole. Thanks, Dad. Thanks a whole hell of a lot.

(A pause. LAWRENCE stands, digs in his suitcase, pulls out a beach towel and a swim suit and exits.)

(MATTHEW pounds the trash can two or three times.)

(Lights fade to black.)

END

DUANE & RUFFIE

(Lights up two tall chairs. Seated on the two tall chairs are DUANE and SAMUEL. DUANE wears a muted check suit, a wide tie and sports a fuzzy beard. DUANE has on his right arm a tall wooden box covered in rust-colored shag carpet. On his hand inside the box is RUFFIE DOG, a well-crafted, bright-eyed dog puppet. Seated in the other chair is SAMUEL. SAMUEL wears a tan shirt, brown cords and large glasses. He holds a few loose, spiral bound papers. Both DUANE and SAMUEL wear over-large body microphones.)

SAMUEL
Mr. Andlew, thank you for being here this morning.

DUANE
My pleasure.

SAMUEL
To have both of you, here at the same time --

RUFFIE DOG
Can't have one without the other.

DUANE
Of course.

SAMUEL
I've been watching what the two of you do for years --

DUANE
The riddles and jokes --

SAMUEL
The riddles and jokes --

RUFFIE DOG
"Why did the man put the car in the oven?"

SAMUEL
A riddle like that one --

DUANE
"Because the cake was in the garage."

RUFFIE DOG
"Because the man wanted a "hot-rod.""

DUANE
Either rejoinder works with that specific riddle.

SAMUEL
That's the beauty --

DUANE
Of that specific riddle --

SAMUEL
That's the beauty of the "car in the oven" riddle.

DUANE
It can work with either response.

RUFFIE DOG
Cars are too big to fit into ovens unless the ovens were specially made to cook cars and what regular person would be able to afford an oven that size unless the person was living a lifestyle where money was not an object. And the "hot-rod" retort is a play on words, in that if one were to cook a car, said car would become "hot" and a slang term for a fast car is the term "hot-rod." Thus the wordplay.

(A pause.)

SAMUEL
Mr. Andlew, your backstory --

DUANE
-- I had difficult period, yes --

SAMUEL
-- tough times a number of years ago --

DUANE
-- It was a difficult period for me --

SAMUEL
-- yes --

DUANE
-- it was actually a good lesson --

SAMUEL
-- the bad times you endured --

DUANE
-- it's been years since the bad times --

SAMUEL
It's a good story for the children --

DUANE
A story for them relate to, yes, something for children to help them get a sense of the lessons of life, something that might aid with decisions they can make as they get older when I talk about the bad, terrible things that happened to me and that I was awful things I was involved with.

SAMUEL
And you freely talk about those things.

DUANE
Yes. When asked specifically to do so.

SAMUEL
Tell us a little about the fun excitement that's coming up for you and Ruffie this week.

DUANE
This week is our annual visit to the state fair.

SAMUEL
Every year --

DUANE
-- every year we are at the fair, Ruffie and I host a talent competition --

SAMUEL

Who judges the talent?

DUANE

Ruffie is the judge.

RUFFIE DOG

I have a keen eye for good talent.

SAMUEL

What are some of your criteria?

RUFFIE DOG

"Criteria?"

DUANE

(to RUFFIE DOG) He means on what basis do you judge the competitors?

SAMUEL

-- oh, I'm sorry, on what basis do you judge the competitors?

RUFFIE DOG

I judge them on basic talent.

SAMUEL

Could you be more specific?

RUFFIE DOG

If there is someone who is good at hoola-hooping, then I judge them on that.

SAMUEL

Compared to --

RUFFIE DOG

Past and present hoola-hoopers from past state fair competitions.

SAMUEL

Have you seen many hoola-hoopers in competition over the years?

RUFFIE DOG

How many?

SAMUEL
Can you ascertain the number you've seen?

RUFFIE DOG
"Ascertain?"

DUANE
Deduce.

RUFFIE DOG
Millions.

SAMUEL
A fair number of hula-hoopers.

DUANE
Mostly we very much enjoy the crowds who come to visit, so if you're watching and you're stopping at the state fair, come by and see our shows at noon and three-thirty on the Orange-Delta Stage between 4-H and Cattle Judging.

SAMUEL
I don't need to tell everyone that the talent show is a great show to watch. Everyone has seen your show and anyone who hasn't, they should know it's a great show. I don't understand how they couldn't have seen it or how they could not know that already that it's great.

DUANE
Come on down the fair for the fun.

(A pause.)

SAMUEL
How long have you been on the air now here with us at channel thirteen?

DUANE
Eighteen years.

SAMUEL
A long time.

DUANE
Eighteen years.

SAMUEL
You've both been watched by parents and children alike.

DUANE
Yes.

SAMUEL
You two are practically immortal.

DUANE
I don't know if I'd go as far as to say that.

SAMUEL
Both you and Ruffie will live on in trillions of young people's collective consciousnesses.

RUFFIE DOG
Grrr -- ruff ruff!

SAMUEL
Someday, possibly twenty or thirty years from now, when Duane Aldlew is dead and Ruffie Dog is in his beaten and loosely packed suitcase, finally abandoned and discarded in a prop bin somewhere in a back room at our downtown studio, on that day there will be a mental uprising, a gathering of hallucinations and memory that will focus on a face, a bearded face and a dog, a silly dog, and this mental conglomeration will form a vast bubble in our shared thinking, a bubble that will be both sad and joyous -- sad because both of you will have been by then deeply and cataclysmically forgotten but also joyous in our minute remembering of the fun times you both brought to the day-to-day of everyone you affected through your joint television appearances, your raucous talent shows at the state fair and your never ceasing need to make us all feel good and happy and chuckle here and there some for a little while, too. (pause) We have a short clip --

DUANE
This should give folks an idea --

SAMUEL
This is, I believe --

DUANE
-- a clip of last year's state fair appearance --

SAMUEL
This will give people an idea regarding what I spoke of --

DUANE
-- this is what it's like at the fair with Duane and Ruffie.

SAMUEL
Duane and Ruffie at the state fair. Let's watch.

(A very long, silent pause as DUANE and SAMUEL watch a blinking side monitor until the clip ends.)

SAMUEL
We didn't have sound here in the studio, but, Duane, you could probably tell what was
happening on the monitor --

DUANE
Just as I described, it was last year at the state fair with us --

SAMUEL
-- the state fair. It's fun. (beat) (to camera) So make it out next week to the fair if you can to see Duane and Ruffie, hosting two shows --

RUFFIE DOG
Noon and three-thirty.

SAMUEL
Noon and three-thirty.

RUFFIE DOG
At the Orange-Delta Stage.

SAMUEL
The Orange-Delta Stage. Bring your hula-hoop, those who aspire for winning. (beat) Would you both be so kind to do us one last favor?

DUANE
Of course.

SAMUEL
A final, quick "Where's Ruffie?"

(A beat. RUFFIE DOG sinks into the box. A beat.)

SAMUEL

(to the box) Where's Ruffie!?!

(RUFFIE DOG pops out of the box.)

RUFFIE DOG

Here I am!

(A pause.)

SAMUEL

Wonderful.

(A pause. Lights out.)

END

www.ingramcontent.com/pod-product-compliance
Ingram Content Group UK Ltd.
Pitfield, Milton Keynes, MK11 3LW, UK
UKHW020127250726
13967UKWH00002B/527

9 780557 867288